THE UNIVERSE

ASTEROIDS, COMETS, AND METEOROIDS

ABDO
Publishing Company

A Buddy Book **by** Fran Howard

VISIT US AT
www.abdopublishing.com

Published by ABDO Publishing Company, 8000 West 78th Street, Edina, Minnesota 55439.

Printed in the United States.

Editor: Sarah Tieck
Contributing Editor: Michael P. Goecke
Graphic Design: Maria Hosley
Cover Image: Lushpix
Interior Images: Library of Congress (page 21); Lushpix (page 13, 15, 23, 28, 29); NASA: Jet Propulsion Laboratory (page 9, 11, 25, 27), Johnson Space Center (page 29); Photos.com (page 5, 19, 30).

Library of Congress Cataloging-in-Publication Data

Howard, Fran, 1953-
  Asteroids, comets, and meteoroids / Fran Howard.
    p. cm. — (The universe)
  Includes index.
  ISBN 978-1-59928-925-0
  1. Asteroids—Juvenile literature. 2. Comets—Juvenile literature. 3. Meteoroids—Juvenile literature. I. Title.

  QB651.H69 2008
  523.44--dc22
                        2007027793

Table Of Contents

Asteroids, Comets, And Meteoroids

When people look up into the night sky, they can see the moon and the stars. Sometimes, they can even see planets glowing brightly.

These space objects are just a few parts of our solar system. Asteroids, comets, and meteoroids are part of our solar system, too.

Every so often, it is possible to see one in the night sky. Some people have even seen them during the day!

People usually don't see asteroids and comets. But, meteoroids are often seen in our night sky. We call them shooting stars.

Our Solar System

A solar system is a star with space objects, such as planets, orbiting it. Our sun is the center of our solar system.

Earth is one of eight planets that orbit our sun. The other planets are Mercury, Venus, Mars, Jupiter, Saturn, Uranus, and Neptune. Dwarf planets, such as Pluto, also orbit the sun.

Saturn
Uranus
Jupiter
Earth
Venus
Mercury

Kuiper Belt

Scientists say that asteroids, comets, and meteoroids come from a few specific parts of space. These are the asteroid belt, the Kuiper belt, and the Oort cloud.

Some planets have moons. Scientists have discovered more than 100 moons in our solar system. Asteroids, comets, and meteoroids are smaller than all of these space objects!

7

A Closer Look

Asteroids are big space rocks. They can be many shapes. Some are the size of large boulders. Others are miles across.

Comets are a mix of rock and frozen gases. Some have long tails made of gas and dust.

Meteoroids are rock and dust **particles** in space. When a meteoroid enters Earth's **atmosphere**, it either burns up or hits Earth. If a meteoroid hits Earth, it is called a meteorite.

The comet *(above left)* and asteroid *(below)* are pictured in space. The meteorite *(above right)* was found on Earth. Worldwide, people have found more than 22,000 meteorites.

Asteroids

Asteroids are sometimes called minor planets or planetoids. Not all asteroids have names. In fact, many only have numbers.

Some asteroids have moons. And, scientists think some asteroids orbit planets. These are called captured asteroids. Scientists believe Mars's moons, Phobos and Deimos, may be captured asteroids.

Ida

Ida's moon

Ida is an asteroid. Photographs from the *Galileo* spacecraft helped scientists discover that it has a moon.

Most asteroids orbit the sun in the asteroid belt. This is the part of space between Mars and Jupiter. There may be more than 1 million asteroids larger than one-half mile (1 km) across!

Some scientists think a planet once existed where the asteroid belt is now. They think the asteroids could be debris from this planet.

Comets

A comet's body is round like a snowball. It forms when **debris** (duh-BREE) and gases mix together and then freeze.

The pressure of sunlight and solar wind creates streams of dust behind the comet. This is the comet's tail.

A comet's body is usually smaller than 12 miles (19 km) across. Its tail can be many times bigger than its body!

Some comets are bright enough to be viewed from Earth. These comets can be seen when they pass by the planet. Others can be seen only through telescopes.

Comets are found throughout our solar system. There are long-period comets, which can take more than 1,000 years to orbit the sun.

There are also short-period comets. These take less than 200 years to complete an oval-shaped orbit.

Scientists think most long-period comets come from a part of space called the Oort cloud. This is in the outer solar system.

Scientists believe short-period comets form in the Kuiper belt. This area is located beyond Neptune.

A comet's tail always points away from the sun. This means a comet's body approaches the sun first. A comet moves away from the sun tail first.

Meteoroids

Meteoroids are smaller than asteroids. They are pieces of rock and dust floating in space.

Most meteoroids burn up when they enter Earth's **atmosphere**. These are called meteors, fireballs, or shooting stars.

Meteoroids that don't burn up can damage a planet's surface. Meteoroids are called meteorites when they hit a planet.

Meteoroids can hit hard enough to make deep, bowl-shaped holes called craters. This meteorite crater in Arizona is 4,180 feet (1,275 m) wide and 570 feet (174 m) deep!

Space Discoveries

People have been aware of shooting stars and comets for many years. But comets appear and disappear suddenly in the sky. Because of this, some ancient people were afraid of comets. Some even thought comets brought bad luck!

Gottfried Kirch discovered the great comet of 1680. This was the first comet to be seen through a telescope. A great comet is bright and can be seen easily. However, a great comet appears only about once every 10 years.

Years ago, people gathered to watch comets. The great comet of 1882 was very bright. It could be seen from Earth during the day without a telescope. The great daylight comet of 1910 was even brighter!

In the early 1800s, scientists began studying asteroids. Ceres was the first asteroid to be discovered. Today, scientists consider Ceres a dwarf planet.

From 1801 to 1807, scientists discovered four additional asteroids. For many years, scientists believed there were no more asteroids because they could not find any.

By 1845, scientists began to discover new asteroids again. And by the 1980s, scientists had discovered several thousand asteroids.

In recent years, scientists have become concerned that an asteroid could crash into Earth. So in the late 1990s, they created a computer to help them discover asteroids.

Our solar system has an asteroid belt. In recent years, scientists have found more than 1 million asteroids!

Missions Into Space

In 2005, the United States **launched** the Deep Impact **mission**. A **spacecraft** was sent into space with a smaller spacecraft attached to it. The smaller craft was sent to crash into comet Tempel 1. It was called the impactor.

The *Deep Impact* impactor left a large crater where it hit the comet. The *Deep Impact* spacecraft collected dust and **debris** from the comet for scientists to study.

When *Deep Impact* crashed into comet Tempel 1, it left a large crater. It also damaged the impactor.

The Deep Impact **mission** was sent directly to Tempel 1. Other missions have studied comets while traveling to other space objects.

The *Near Earth Asteroid Rendezvous (NEAR) Shoemaker* was the first **spacecraft** sent directly to an asteroid. This U.S. **mission** was **launched** to study Eros. Eros is the second-largest asteroid close to Earth.

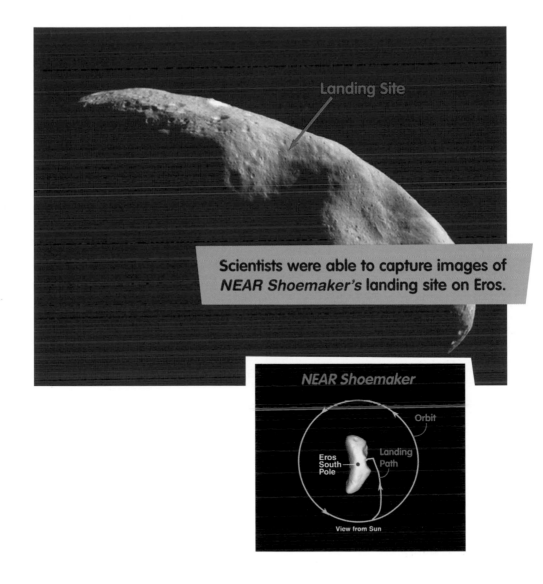

Landing Site

Scientists were able to capture images of *NEAR Shoemaker's* landing site on Eros.

NEAR Shoemaker

Orbit

Eros
South
Pole

Landing
Path

View from Sun

Fact Trek

Halley's comet can be seen from Earth every 75 or 76 years. It passed near Earth in 1986 and will reappear in 2061.

Halley's comet is a short-period comet.

Some scientists think a large meteorite caused the great dinosaur **extinction**.

Comets can change if they pass too close to planets or the sun. The sun's heat can melt comets. And, planets can knock them out of the solar system!

The sun's heat can change a comet's shape. If the comet melts, it may disappear completely!

Voyage To Tomorrow

Scientists study asteroids, comets, and meteoroids for many reasons. In 2014, an international **spacecraft** called *Rosetta* will enter the orbit of comet 67P. And from 2011 to 2015, the U.S. *Dawn* spacecraft is expected to orbit the asteroid Vesta.

Some scientists think asteroids could be a source of minerals like those found on Earth. They hope to use the minerals some day.

Important Words

atmosphere the layer of gases that surrounds space objects, including planets, moons, and stars.

debris the remains of something that has been broken or destroyed.

extinction when living things die out, so none are left.

launch to send off with great force.

mission the sending of spacecraft to perform specific jobs.

particle a small piece or part.

spacecraft a vehicle that travels in space.

Web Sites

To learn more about **asteroids, comets, and meteoroids**, visit ABDO Publishing Company on the World Wide Web. Web sites about **asteroids, comets, and meteoroids** are featured on our Book Links page. These links are routinely monitored and updated to provide the most current information available.

www.abdopublishing.com

INDEX